18th & 19th CENTURY
WORKS

THOEMMES

Printed in Great Britain by
Antony Rowe Ltd, Chippenham, Wiltshire

REMARKS
ON MR. HUME'S
DIALOGUES CONCERNING
NATURAL RELIGION

Thomas Hayter

With a new Introduction by
John Valdimir Price

THOEMMES PRESS

© Thoemmes Press 1992

Published in 1992 by
Thoemmes Press
85 Park Street
Bristol BS1 5PJ
England

ISBN 1 85506 178 3

This is a reprint of the 1780 Edition

Publisher's Note

INTRODUCTION

'No virtuous father will ever recommend them to the perusal of his son, except in point of composition; and every impartial judge must pronounce them unworthy of a writer of such distinguished abilities as Mr. HUME.'[1] So wrote William Rose at the conclusion of his notice of David Hume's *Dialogues concerning Natural Religion* in the November 1779 issue of *The Monthly Review*. Since Rose had commented favourably on some of Hume's other publications, his hostility to the *Dialogues* is a little surprising, but it may have had something to do with the trouble Hume took to be sure that the work would be published posthumously and the various difficulties that ensued in bringing about the publication of the book after Hume's death. Shortly before Rose's review appeared, Hume's good friend, Hugh Blair, had asserted in a letter of 3 August 1779 to William Strahan: 'as to D. Hume's Dialogues, I am surprised that though they have been published for some time, they have made so little noise. They are exceedingly elegant. They bring together some of his most exceptionable reasonings; but the principles themselves were all in his former works'.[2] Blair's remarks, as one can see, were a little

---

[1] *The Monthly Review* (London: R. Griffiths, 1780), LXI, 355.

[2] Edinburgh University Library, MS. Dc. 2. 76[10]. Cited in John Valdimir Price, ed., David Hume: *Dialogues concerning Natural Religion* (Oxford: The Clarendon Press, 1976), p. 121. Subsequent quotations from the *Dialogues* are from this edition, with page numbers cited in text.

premature, and the work attracted reviews or notices in various journals and was the subject of a good deal of comment in several books. The contention by the German historian Frederick August Wendeborn that the *Dialogues* 'created more noise abroad than they did in England'[3] may be correct, but the continental reception of Hume's *Dialogues* is not a subject that has elicited much scholarly attention.

The crucial period for the early reception and reputation of the work would have been between its publication, in two separate editions, in 1779, and its incorporation into Hume's collected works in the 1788 edition of his *Essays and Treatises on Several Subjects*. It was not included in the 1784 edition of the *Essays and Treatises*, so it is perhaps not unreasonable to infer that copies of the first or second edition remained in print until 1788. The first edition, published in Edinburgh, probably consisted of no more than the 500 copies that Hume had mentioned among his sundry instructions about the publication, and the second edition was probably about a thousand copies. It is this second edition from which all the responders to the work quote.[4] Since Hume had arranged with his nephew to have copies of the first printing presented to a number of his friends, it is possible that very few copies of this edition were available for sale.

---

[3] Frederick August Wendeborn, *A View of England towards the Close of the Eighteenth Century* (Dublin: William Sleater, 1791), II, 339. This is Wendeborn's own translation of his German original, *Der Zustand des Staats der Religion, der Gelehrsamkeit und der Kunst in Grossbritannien* (Berlin: Bey and Spener, 1785-88), where he had said of the *Dialogues* that it was 'hier bei weitem das Aussehen nicht verurfachten, welches sie in Deutschland gemacht haben söllen. Sie sind hier bereits vergessen' (III, 365).

[4] See my edition of the *Dialogues*, pp. 105-128 for information about the publishing history of the work.

Despite the almost comical piety of William Rose's conclusion, he had, however, begun his review in a more conciliatory manner, describing the *Dialogues* as a 'very elaborate performance...written with great elegance' and in its composition 'equal, if not superior' to any of Hume's lifetime publications. Just as Hugh Blair felt that the work contained nothing new, so did Rose, saying that Hume had largely taken some of his more objectionable doctrines and cast them in a 'new form' in order to 'present them in a different dress.' As with many eighteenth-century reviews, Rose's consists of large chunks of quotation, and in the twelve pages devoted to the work he makes a number of valid and interesting comments about the *Dialogues*, but does ask 'what gratitude is due to Mr. Hume for this legacy to the public?'[5]

James Beattie had very much the same attitude towards the *Dialogues*, even to the extent of anticipating Rose's vocabulary when he wrote, in a letter of 15 July 1777, to the Duchess of Gordon, that 'the world is now in the possession of Mr Hume's Legacy'. Beattie also took the opportunity to charge Hume once again with atheism. Noting the lengths that Hume went to in order to safeguard the posthumous publication of the work, he says that Adam Smith 'to do him credit, refused to have any thing to do with it,' that Hume's printer, William Strahan, 'refused to print it,' and, unbelievably, that George III 'was said to have signified his desire, that it might be suppressed'. That the work was eventually published through the efforts of Hume's nephew, also David

Hume, is well-established,[6] but it provides the occasion for Beattie to sneer that Hume had 'bequeathed his whole fortune, both in money and atheism' to this 'brisk young man'.[7] The charge of atheism was one that Hume endured all his life: even Henry Home, Lord Kames, Hume's friend and mentor, who ought to have known better, told James Boswell, on 4 December 1782, shortly before he died, that, 'David's atheism was owing to his want of sensibility. He did not perceive the benevolence of the Deity in His works'.[8] Whether Kames was well enough to read the *Dialogues*, or indeed had discussed it with Hume in the 1750s when Hume first began drafting the work is not documented. Boswell would have had occasion to find out when he was visiting Kames on 25 January 1780, and they were joined by Hume's nephew. Boswell records that he was highly offended by 'his publishing his uncle's poison', but there is no evidence to suggest that Boswell had bothered to read the work.[9]

Contemporary analyses of the *Dialogues* often turned upon correlations between the views of Hume and Philo, as well as Hume's reputation as a philosopher and his character as a human being.

---

[6] Even James Beattie was better informed than Hume's first biographer, Thomas Edward Ritchie, who wrote in his *Account of the Life and Writings of David Hume* (London: Cadell and Davies, 1807), that the *Dialogues* was 'published under the superintendence of Dr. Adam Smith' (p. 301).

[7] Cited in *Dialogues*, p. 124, from the Forbes (Fettercairn) papers now in the National Library of Scotland.

[8] *Boswell: The Applause of the Jury, 1782-1785*, ed. Irma S. Lustig and Frederick A. Pottle (London: Heinemann, 1982), p. 31.

[9] *Boswell, Laird of Auchinlech, 1778-1782*, ed. Joseph W. Reed and Frederick A. Pottle (New York: McGraw-Hill, 1977), p. 173.

Those who did comment on the characters invariably regarded Philo as the spokesman for Hume. William Rose, in his *Monthly Review* notice, ladled out both approval and disapproval of the work as a whole, but did not specifically link Philo's views to Hume. He felt that Cleanthes defended a 'good cause very feebly,' but could not be called an 'accurate philosopher,' while Demea 'supports the character of a sour, croaking divine, very tolerably'. Philo was, however, 'the hero of the piece' who 'urges his objections with no inconsiderable degree of acuteness and subtlety'.[10] Rose was thus at least aware of the work as a structured narrative and left it to his readers to make any inferences that they might with respect to the 'real-life' identity of the characters. Similarly, the reviewer in *The Gentleman's Magazine* quotes Pamphilus' description to Hermippus of Philo, Cleanthes, and Demea but associates the views of Philo and perhaps Cleanthes with other writers: 'We need not say on which side this sceptical metaphysician inclines the balance, but must observe, that the weapons with which Philo attracts [sic] the moral attributes of the Deity are the same with those employed by Lord Bolingbroke, and were most ably parried by Bishop Warburton.'[11] The *Gentleman's Magazine* reviewer could possibly be alluding to some of Hume's publications in the 1750s and the controversy they generated. For example, when the first volume of his *History of England* was published in 1754, Hume wrote to the Earl of Balcarres to say that the 'weekly papers have been busy with me,' making

---

[10] *The Monthly Review*, LXI (1780), 343.

[11] *The Gentleman's Magazine* (London: D. Henry, 1779), XLIX, 508.

him 'as great an atheist as Bolingbroke'.[12] He had
described Warburton as a 'low Fellow' (*Letters*, I,
250), probably in response to Warburton's author-
ship, along with Richard Hurd, of an attack on Hume
entitled *Remarks on Mr David Hume's Essay on the
Natural History of Religion* (1757).

Joseph Priestley rather curiously identified Demea
as 'the orthodox speaker,' rather than Cleanthes in his
Letters to a Philosophical Unbeliever (1780) and
joined James Beattie in implying that Hume is to be
numbered among the atheists rather than theists or
doubters. Priestley assures the 'philosophical unbeliever'
to whom his *Letters* are addressed that the work 'is
frequently a topic of conversation in the societies you
frequent,' but since these putative societies are
nowhere identified in the book, one has to take this
assertion as a bit of rhetorical flummery. He finds
the work 'ingeniously and artfully constructed', and
that Philo 'evidently speaks the sentiments of the
writer', but without being 'made to say all the good
things that are advanced'; while Philo's 'opponents are
not made to say any thing that is very palpably
absurd, and every thing is made to pass with great
decency and decorum'. In light of this remark, one
wonders how sensitively or carefully Priestley read the
Dialogues, since it is clear from the rhetorical
structure and texture of some of Demea's remarks
that Hume is making him say things that the reader is
invited to perceive as palpably absurd.

It is difficult to tell if Priestley's alarm at the so-
called 'atheistical' nature of the work is real or

---

[12] *The Letters of David Hume*, ed. J.Y.T. Greig (Oxford: The Clarendon
Press, 1932), I, 214. Hereafter cited in text as *Letters*, with relevant
volume and page numbers.

feigned. In the last part of our secular and secularizing twentieth century, it is perhaps impossible to believe the hostility with which God-fearing folk of an earlier time regarded any words which might have contained or sustained the slightest doubt about the veracity of the Christian gospel. Priestley seems to perceive dangers in the work where none exist:

> And though the debate seemingly closes in favour of the theist, the victory is clearly on the side of the atheist. I shall therefore not be surprised if this work should have a considerable effect in promoting the cause of atheism, with those whose *general turn of thinking*, and *habits of life*, make them no ill-wishers to that scheme.[13]

There is, alas, no record of Priestley's recording his surprise when, in fact, the work had no success whatsoever in 'promoting the cause of atheism'.

The reviewer in *The Critical Review* for September, 1779, did not raise the question of atheism, avoids linking the views of Hume's characters to any specific person, living or dead, and begins the review with compliments to Hume and liberal assertions about free enquiry. Opening with a tribute to Hume's well-known 'great abilities' and contending that the reader will find in 'these Dialogues the profoundest researches, and the most acute reasoning', the reviewer savers any fears that the 'friends of religion' might have about the harm the *Dialogues* could do, or the possible triumph that religion's enemies might feel are both groundless: 'Freedom of enquiry can never be injurious to the cause of truth.' Truth may not be

---

[13] Joseph Priestley, *Letters to a Philosophical Unbeliever* (Bath: Cruttwell, 1780), pp. 105, 108-109. Hereafter cited in text as Priestley.

injured by free enquiry, but it seems the stability of mankind might be were Hume's principles inculcated among the generality of mankind. Although Hume is described as 'ingenious', 'sagacious', and 'animated', the reviewer feels that Hume's views would 'throw a gloom over the whole creation, and really terminate in the blind amazement, the diffidence and melancholy of mankind'. Philo's objections to natural religion were not advanced modestly, Cleanthes apparently is not permitted to answer them as fully as a natural theologian would be capable of doing, and Philo's tone of 'triumph and defiance' lends to the work 'the aspect of infidelity'.[14] Hume had, to be sure, become inured to charges of atheism and infidelity long before his death in 1776, so nothing in those comments would have surprised him.

Like other reviewers, the one for *The Critical Review* exhibits a certain amount of familiarity with Hume's writings, and one of the strengths of the review is its apparent open-mindedness. What is absent from most of these commentaries is any sense of the drama of what is taking place in the *Dialogues* or any perception, much less appreciation, of the give-and-take in the exchange of views, or of the tentativeness of the conclusion that is reached. In his other writings, Hume had repeatedly emphasized the pleasures of philosophical reasoning as an activity of the mind. Even when his inquiries produced no epistemological or moral imperatives, or failed to give

---

[14] *The Critical Review* (London: A. Hamilton, 1779), XLVIII, 161, 171. It is perhaps worth recording that the reviewer of another of Hume's works published posthumously, his *Essays on Suicide, and the Immortality of the Soul* (London: M. Smith, 1783) used almost the same phrase to describe the effect of Hume's principles as having a tendency 'to cast a gloom over the whole creation' (*The Critical Review*, 1783), LVI, 475.

him, or his readers, the certitude that he or they might have desired, the 'gloomy' conclusions that he reached did not impair either his sociability or his good humour. Early readers seem tempted to search the text for a stick to beat Hume with and seem puzzled or surprised that they could do so only when they imputed a one-to-one correspondence between the sentiments of Philo and those of Hume.

That Hume seemed to have as his object the extirpation of religion in general and the Christian religion in particular is a feature of several of the contemporary responses to the *Dialogues*. The Aberdonian philosopher, John Ogilvie, in his *Inquiry into the Cause of Infidelity and Scepticism of the Times* (1783), asserted that the *Dialogues* was an 'attempt to exterminate the religious principle altogether', and implied that Philo was more of an atheist than not: 'As Philo's declarations upon this subject [belief in a deity] are contradictory, I construct his notions most favourably, when I consider him as excluding a Deity from the universe.'[15] It seems idle to note Philo's asseveration in Part 2 of the *Dialogues* that 'the Question can never be concerning the *Being* but only the *Nature* of the Deity', although the manner in which he says this and its context may validate Pamphilus' earlier suspicion that Cleanthes had 'perceiv'd some Raillery or artificial Malice in the Reasonings of *Philo*' (*Dialogues*, pp. 160, 148). Philo's declarations of belief in a deity, or in some correlation between the causes of order in the universe

[15] John Ogilvie, *An Inquiry into the Causes of Infidelity and Scepticism of the Times: With Occasional Observations on The Writings of Herbert, Shaftesbury, Bolingbroke, Hume, Gibbon, Toulmin, &c. &c.* (London: Richardson and Urquhart, 1783), pp. 335n., 68n. Hereafter cited in text as Ogilvie.

and human intelligence may need to be treated with caution and examined for irony or 'Raillery', but there seems little doubt that, at least for the sake of the discussion, he does not absolutely exclude a deity from his account of the universe.

These contemporary commentaries, and others, on the *Dialogues* frequently turned upon the character of the author, and many were convinced that Hume was second only to Beelzebub in his enmity to religion. William Rose, in his *Monthly Review* notice, is clearly somewhat puzzled by Hume's determination to see that his work was published after his death. Hume had, he contends, 'long been floating on the boundless and pathless ocean of scepticism', but the *Dialogues* goes beyond what can be explained by his self-acknowledged desire for literary fame and his love of paradox. Rose is either confused or ambivalent about the work, since he seems to feel, on the one hand, that the work contains nothing new and therefore cannot be any more theologically offensive than any of Hume's previous writings; and, on the other hand, that only the 'giddy, the profligate, and the unprincipled' would be confirmed in their 'prejudices against religion and virtue' by a perusal of the work: it would be 'despised by every man who has the smallest grain of seriousness and reflection'. Rose can find no real explanation for its publication, except to repeat that Hume's love of paradox and literary fame was so overweening that it continued after his death; he is genuinely perplexed that Hume would want to publish a work that 'must shock the sense and virtue' of his fellow human beings; nor is his desire to have it published capable of being reconciled with his reputation as a 'good citizen and friend to mankind'.[16] Since Hume was not alive to respond to these admonitory strictures, they seem to be more rhetorical gestures than anything else, perhaps directed obliquely at the publisher and those of Hume's friends involved in the posthumous publication.

Joseph Priestley takes a rather stronger line and draws on Hume's first authorized publication after his death, his autobiography, *The Life of David Hume, Esq. Written by Himself* (1777), to reinforce his hostility to Hume. Referring to this work, Priestley confesses that he is 'surprised to find no mention of a *God*, or of a *providence*' in the *Dialogues*, but adds that such an omission 'cannot be any longer wonderful, when we find that for any thing he certainly believed to the contrary, he himself might be the most remarkable being in the universe'. Alluding facetiously but maliciously to some of Philo's more imaginative speculations about the origin of the universe, he asserts that Hume's 'maker, if he had any, was either a careless playful infant, a trifling forgetful dotard, or was, perhaps, dead and buried, without leaving any other to take care of his affairs'. Equating Hume's and Philo's beliefs, he concludes of Hume 'All that he believed of his maker was, that he was capable of *something like design*, but of his own comprehensive intellectual powers he could have no doubt' (Priestley, p. 116). Priestley evidently never read Hume's *Treatise*.[17]

[16] *The Monthly Review*, LXI, 354,355.

[17] The reviewer of Priestley's book in *The Critical Review* for October, 1780 (volume 50) quickly perceived the bitter personalism of Priestley's examination, saying that he expressed 'the most contemptuous opinion of Mr. Hume... and seems to think that he could not have maintained so many absurdities, if he had given himself the trouble to read Dr. Hartley's "Observations on Man"' (p. 241).

Priestley's rather heavy-handed cavilling is not
much different from the kind of analysis and abuse
that Hume received in his lifetime from those who felt
that his views totally subverted Christianity and therefore the structure of the universe. Much of the
criticism becomes tedious and repetitive, and while
Hume offered his views as those of an impartial or
disinterested observer or commentator, many readers
could respond only with hostility or incredulity, or
both, to his representations of religion, Christian or
otherwise. So it is refreshing to come across an
occasional rejoinder to the *Dialogues*, in which Hume
is treated humorously, even ironically; and when the
author proves to be the Bishop of Norwich, George
Horne, the humour is doubly welcome.

Horne's first printed comment on Hume was in
effect a reply to Adam Smith's letter to Hume's
publisher, William Strahan, which was printed in
Hume's posthumous autobiography. In the same year,
Horne published, anonymously, a witty response, *A
Letter to Adam Smith. On the Life, Death, and
Philosophy of his Friend David Hume. By One of the
People called Christians.* Although Horne's humour
often verges on sarcasm, he is probably commenting
more effectively on Hume's posthumous reputation as
heretic than some of the more serious and heavy-
handed writers. After the publication in 1779 of the
Dialogues and, in 1783, an edition of Hume's
suppressed *Essays on Suicide, and the Immortality of
the Soul,*[18] Horne published his *Letters on Infidelity*.
Beginning with a clever analogy between the

---

[18] See the reprint, with my introduction, of Hume's *Essays on Suicide, and
the Immortality of the Soul* (London: Smith, 1783), published also by
Thoemmes Press, 1992

Dialogues and a pudding, Horne constituted his response to the *Dialogues* with his own 'Dialogue Between Thomas and Timothy on Philosophical Scepticism'. Horne's dialogue opens with a citation of Philo's enigmatic concluding assertion that 'To be a philosophical Sceptic is, in a man of Letters, the first and most essential Step towards being a sound, believing Christian' (*Dialogues*, p. 261). Timothy replies to this that 'One thing is certain, that if scepticism be the road to Christianity, Mr. H. is a very proper person to keep the turnpike gate upon it'.[19] Most of the dialogue proceeds in this ironic way and very effectively deploys Hume's chosen literary form, the dialogue, against him. One feels at the very least that Horne detected the slyness and impishness of the humour in the *Dialogues* and decided to respond in kind.

John Ogilvie's assessment of Hume is neither so witty as that of Horne, nor so judgmental as that of Priestley, perhaps in deference to a fellow Scot. Although he regarded the *Dialogues* as a 'shocking compound of absurdity and blasphemy', he expressed a desire to do justice to Hume's character and his writings, regarding the latter 'as models of correct and classical composition'. As for Hume himself, Ogilvie felt that his 'talents were undoubtedly of the first rate. And that they have failed to guard him from the charges of inconsistence and of absurdity, we must ascribe to his carrying the love of paradox, and of singular argument into the dangerous sphere of religion' (Ogilvie, p. 70n.). Ogilvie is, of course, alluding to Philo's comment at the beginning of Part

---

[19] George Horne, *Letters on Infidelity* (Oxford: Clarendon Press, 1784), p. 5.

12 of the *Dialogues* about his 'Love of singular
Arguments' (*Dialogues*, p. 245).

Although Ogilvie had linked Hume, Gibbon,
infidelity, and scepticism on his title-page, the first
author to link Hume and Gibbon was Joseph Milner
in 1781, *Gibbon's Account of Christianity
Considered, Together with some Strictures on Hume's
Dialogues concerning Natural Religion.*[20] Most of the
book is given over to an examination of the fifteenth
and sixteenth chapters of the first volume (1776) of
Gibbon's *History of the Decline and Fall of the
Roman Empire*, but Milner considers Hume's
Dialogues and some of his other views on religion,
morality, and conscience towards the end of his book.
Milner, too, lightens his personal attack on Hume
with a little humour. At the end of the *Dialogues*,
Hume alludes to 'that Gloom and Melancholy, so
remarkable in all devout People' (p. 259). Milner
takes up this comment, saying that he had spent a
great deal of time in the company of the devout and
had invariably found them cheerful, particularly in the
face of death, 'But I can conceive how the reserve and
awe, which the accidental company of a man so
horribly impious and so profoundly sagacious as Mr.
Hume might strike a pious mind, would by him be
construed into melancholy' (Milner, p. 126). Despite
Milner's uncertain syntax, he at least relieves his
general personal condemnation of Hume with a little
levity. Like Priestley, Milner is certain that Philo
speaks for Hume, despite the conclusion in favour of
Cleanthes, 'the natural religionist'; but Philo is the

---

[20] Published by A. Ward in York, 1781. Reprinted by Thoemmes Press,
1989. Cited in text hereafter as Milner, with quotations from the
reprint.

author's 'favourite. Sincerity constitutes no part of a philosopher's virtue.' Milner and Priestley are almost the only contemporary commentators to make any mention of Demea, and Milner's comment is just that, a mention: he has taken no notice of Demea, 'because I cannot find a feature of Christianity about him. Dr. Clark's metaphysicks and the Gospel have, I think, no sort of connection' (Milner, pp. 199, 221). Milner's implied conjunction between the views of Samuel Clarke and those of Demea is one that has persisted.

Milner's observations on Hume and the *Dialogues* have to be seen in terms of the general tenor of the whole book, which is that morality and religion are rapidly losing ground to vice and infidelity and that the moral structure of the world is getting worse day by day. For example, the Pope 'has lost his throne in the eyes of men of sense'; speaking of the clergy he asks, 'Who does not see what an increase of wickedness has prevailed among us'; in the universities the 'neglect of true theological knowledge among the students is palpable'; and, finally, 'that we are a selfish, profane, licentious people is evident' (pp. 238, 254, 255). This apocalyptic vision of Britain in the last quarter of the eighteenth century might be thought to have undermined the seriousness with which Milner's views were considered, but in fact his book was frequently reprinted. Its condemnation of Hume and the *Dialogues* seems merely to reflect a recurring paranoia about one's own time and a nostalgia for a Golden Age that never existed.

Although Thomas Hayter's *Remarks on Mr. Hume's Dialogues concerning Natural Religion* is not different in kind from the writings of other early responders to Hume's *Dialogues*, it is certainly different in degree. He does not articulate the alarmist, hyperbolic views or indulge in the lurid rhetoric of either Priestley or Milner, but he is concerned about the pernicious effect that Philo's views could have upon a religious man. Note, however, that it is his practical concern for the effects on a human psyche of an adherence to the views about misery and evil that Philo iterates that most concern Hayter, not Hume's lack of theological sensitivity; this seems especially true of the conclusion of *Remarks* (pp. 63 - 64) when he writes about the sorrow of the religionist, who mopes under the influence of religion, but who under the guidance of Philo might be likely to commit suicide. Although Hume wrote an essay on suicide that was never published in English during his lifetime, he was not himself made so despondent by his own philosophy that he considered suicide an alternative, which would seem to be the logical implication of Hayter's observation.

Hayter's book attracted at least two notices in the periodical literature of the time. That in *The Monthly Review* is curiously condescending:

> These Remarks are such as must naturally and obviously occur to those readers who are conversant with moral and theological subjects, and acquainted with Mr Hume's writings. They chiefly relate to the moral attributes of the Deity, and the influence of religious principles upon human conduct. The Author writes in a lively and animated manner; and his style, after a little more practice and attention to the rules of composition, will, we doubt not, become more chaste, correct, and uniformly elegant.[21]

[21] *The Monthly Review* (London: R. Griffiths, 1781), LXIV, 159. The comment appears in the Monthly Catalogue for February, 1781.

It is difficult to agree with the reviewer's comment that Hayter's *Remarks* would occur as naturally and obviously as he or she alleges. For one thing, much of the *Dialogues* is devoted to an examination of the argument from design, and another large portion to a discussion of the nature of evil in the universe. Hayter has an effective way of using Philo's own words against him, and while his comments might be construed as natural or obvious rebuttals, his response to Hume is thoughtfully conducted and cogently presented. And in replying to Hume by using his own vocabulary, Hayter is perhaps on stronger ground than many of the other opponents of the views expressed in the *Dialogues*.

The notice in *The Critical Review* accurately summarizes the division of Hayter's book into parts and makes clear that Hayter's purpose is to 'controvert Philo's disavowal of God's moral attributes, and his proscription of popular religion'. Just as many readers of the *Dialogues* seemed to feel that the work was a personal affront to them, the reviewer here congratulates 'our ingenious author' for amply vindicating 'the honour of Christianity'. Quoting Hayter's last paragraph, the reviewer concludes, 'This is a fair stroke, or what the logicians call "argumentum ad hominem", which the advocates of Mr. Hume cannot possibly evade'.[22] Again, one wonders what aspects of Christianity Hume's *Dialogues* could be said to feature: the subject of natural religion would have been anathema to many Christians. One of the strengths of Hayter's *Remarks* is that he does address himself to the issues Philo raises and not to the truth or honour of Christianity.

[22] *The Critical Review* (London: A. Hamilton, 1780), XLIV, 315-316.

Hayter is indeed careful to avoid linking his discussion to any particular form of Christianity and writes about religion in general. The review suggests that the reviewer was more concerned with what Hume's *Dialogues* had the reputation of 'attacking', and not what Hume actually wrote. Hayter, more than most other commentators, tightly and conscientiously confines himself to two major issues in the *Dialogues* and does not spuriously accuse the work of attacking Christianity.

Hayter's book in many ways encapsulates and epitomizes the public perception of Hume and his writings both before and after his death. Reviews and responses to the *Dialogues* acknowledge Hume's literary skills at the same time that they express horror and dismay at some of the views articulated in the work, or, at least, views that readers felt were being articulated. Hume's lifetime reputation as a dangerous infidel frequently interposes itself between the text actually being considered and what the reader imputes to the text. Indeed, Hume himself often becomes the text, and the actual structure and content of the *Dialogues*, its themes and its ideas, are swept aside for speculations about Hume's motives in ensuring the publication of his work.

These reactions cover a fairly wide range of possibilities: bafflement, concern, hostility, admiration, etc., and none of these early commentators on the *Dialogues* gives more than a passing consideration to the dialogue form. Because Philo's words account for about two thirds of the entire text and can often be correlated with specific views in Hume's other texts, it is not surprising that most writers identified Philo as Hume. In his first work, *A Treatise of*

Human Nature, Hume was present in the first person on almost every page, and several reviewers and readers complained about the frequency with which Hume referred to himself. In his last work, Hume seems to have been determined to remove any 'egoisms' from his work and to try to disguise himself as much as possible by employing a literary form that has more in common with narrative fiction than with philosophical treatises or disquisitions. Yet the earliest responders to the *Dialogues* concentrate more on Hume than on the work itself.

In contrast, Thomas Hayter was one of the few authors who addressed himself to some of the serious points raised in the *Dialogues*. Hayter never once directly accuses either Philo or Hume of atheism, for example, nor does he seem unnecessarily concerned with Hume's reputation as an infidel, although the conclusion of his short book measures out his perception of the irreligious import of the *Dialogues*. He challenges Philo's alleged attribution of melancholia and unhappiness exclusively to religion and uses a typically Humean argument against one advanced by Philo: gloomy people would probably be gloomy with or without the assistance or opposition of religion. Perhaps more than any other commentator, Hayter had perceived that the nature of the argument and the way in which it was conducted in the *Dialogues* would have the effect of taking the mystery and metaphysics out of religion and to found it on human happiness. A religious system without an eschatology or a teleology would thus become only a system of morality with some implied supernatural sanction. Hayter ignores what Philo has to say about faith and its role in religious behaviour, but he is replying on empirical grounds to Philo's empirical and experiential charges against religion. In that respect,

Hayter's *Remarks*, while limited in scope, is a genuine, serious, and occasionally sympathetic attempt to answer Hume on his own terms. While it lacks the lightness of touch that Milner occasionally displays and which is one of the salient features of Horne's criticism, it exhibits an awareness of what Hume was trying to do that makes it decidedly different from other early responses to the *Dialogues*.

Extant records indicate that Thomas Hayter was born in March, 1747, in Changford, Devon, the son of the Reverend Joshua Hayter. He was enroled as a schoolboy in Eton. From there, he was admitted, at the age of 18, to King's College, Cambridge, on 25 April 1766. He received his B. A. in 1770 and his M. A. in 1773. He was a fellow of the college from 1769 until his death on 17 December 1799 and is buried in the chapel of King's College.

John Valdimir Price
Honorary Fellow
University of Edinburgh
1992

REMARKS

ON

Mr. HUME's DIALOGUES,

CONCERNING

NATURAL RELIGION.

By T. HAYTER, A.M.

FELLOW OF KING's COLLEGE, CAMBRIDGE;
AND ONE OF THE PREACHERS AT HIS MAJESTY's
CHAPEL IN WHITEHALL.

CAMBRIDGE,

Printed by J. ARCHDEACON, Printer to the
UNIVERSITY;
For T. CADEL, in the Strand, London.
M.DCC.LXXX.

REMARKS

ON

Mr. Hume's DIALOGUES.

Mr. Hume, in the Introduction to his Dialogues (p. 10.) exhibits the following sketch of the personages between whom the Dialogues are supposed to be maintained. "The

"remarkable

" remarkable contraft in their characters
" ftill farther raifed your expectations;
" while you oppofed the accurate philo-
" fophical turn of CLEANTHES to the
" carelefs fcepticifm of PHILO, or com-
" pared either of their difpofitions with
" the rigid inflexible orthodoxy of DE-
" MEA." From this reprefentation one
might at firft be led to look for Mr.
HUME himfelf under the mafk of
CLEANTHES, and to expect from the
mouth of CLEANTHES the celebrated
Metaphyfician's own fentiments. Let
us confider however that Mr. HUME,
after the great nominal fuperiority at-
tributed to CLEANTHES, could not
poffibly, without appearance of vanity,
have appointed CLEANTHES his repre-
fentative. The fact indeed indifputably is, that PHILO, not CLEANTHES,
perfonates Mr. HUME. CLEANTHES
affumes at times (p. 242 and 244) the
tone of DEMEA: while PHILO poffeffes
in general the fole exclufive priviledge
of

of retailing the purport of Mr. Hume's former Philofophical productions.—Every remarkable trait and feature of thofe productions may be traced in the parts of the Dialogue affigned to Philo.

PART

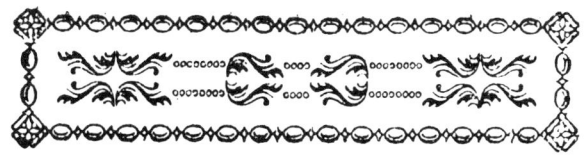

PART I.

THE firſt part of Mr. HUME'S Dialogues is employed in propoſing and canvaſſing different ſyſtems of coſmogony—The ſyſtem of CLEANTHES deducing (p. 47) the univerſe from an intelligent cauſe (after being confronted by various intermediate theorys) is allowed (at p. 196) to prevail over its rivals, and to convert their advocate, PHILO—Neither the ſyſtem of CLEANTHES, in its original ſtate, nor any of its rivals are propoſed

as

PART as the objects of the present disqui-
I.   sition.   The sole aim of these remarks
is to controvert PHILO's own additions
to the system of CLEANTHES, viz.
PHILO's disavowal of God's moral attributes, and his proscription of popular religion.

PHILO's objection to the existence
of benevolence in the divine nature is
grounded principally on the circum-
stance of human misery.   Of this melancholy object he * exhibits (from p.
173 to p. 192.) a most uncomfortable,
forlorn, and, I trust, overcharged description—Some of the darkest shades
in the frightful picture are borrowed
from

---

* I am aware that the topic of human wretched-
ness is (from p. 174 to p. 185.) frequently handled
by DEMEA.   But as the assertions of DEMEA on this
point (from p. 174 to p. 181.) are (at p. 181.) most
cordially assented to by PHILO; and as the remainder
of DEMEA's tragic declamation (down to p. 185.)
meets in that page with a similar warm acquiescence
from his friend; we may surely venture to set down
PHILO a complete proselyte to the dismal creed.

from the Pencils of writers in general, Part
particularly of Poets. Their teftimo-	I.
ny Philo appeals to (p. 173 and 174)
as decifive, "The Poets (p. 173.)
" who fpeak from fentiment, without a
" fyftem, and whofe teftimony has
" therefore more authority, abound in
" images of this nature." Again, (p.
174.) "Look round the library of Cle-
" anthes. I fhall venture to affirm
" that, except authors of particular fci-
" ences fuch as chemiftry and botany,
" who have no occafion to treat of hu-
" man life, there is fcarce one of thofe
" innumerable writers, from whom the
" fenfe of human mifery has not in fome
" paffage or other, extorted a complaint
" and confeffion of it." Let us here, by
Philo's leave, recall to recollection an
old remark "Omnes ingeniofos effe
melancholicos." Suppofe now any
individual of the penfive tribe to la-
bour under a real misfortune or under
the fpleen, and to have, at that critical

moment, a pen in his hand: He inftantly, in all human probability upon
the flighteft provocation in his fubject,
gives a dafh at the condition of mortal
affairs: vents his particular emotions
in general terms: expands a partial
pofture of private concerns into an univerfal reprefentation: and etches a copy
of human life from the prefent complexion of his own fituation—With
refpect to Poets, we need not conceive
them in any actual diftrefs in order
to juftify a fufpicion of fome mifrepre-
fentation in the affair of human cala-
mity. What pathetic incident ever
paffed through the hands of a genuine
bard without receiving many touches
of amplification? And is the interefting
argument of mortal mifery likely to
be difmiffed naked, and unadorned,
totally deftitute of its poetical finifhing?
Without calling in the fuppofition of
abfolute fiction, how greatly does the
warm animated language alone of
poetry

poetry vary the afpect, without altering the circumftances, of a fact; and magnify, without feeming to depart from, truth? In what doth oratory confift? not profeffedly, nor yet vifibly in falfification. Yet, hear the fame identical narrative at one time from an eloquent, at another time from a plain man; you will perceive the one to have heated, you know not why, your paffions and imagination, while the other beft fatisfies your judgement. In a word, the teftimony of authors, efpecially of "the infpired train", as Philo calls the poets, does not feem worthy of the great ftrefs laid upon it by Philo.

Renouncing then the illufions of fancy, let us liften to Philo's own reprefentation of the horrid fcene. "You "afcribe (p. 186) Cleanthes, (and, I "believe, juftly) a purpofe and intenti- "on to nature. But what, I befeech you, "is

Part
I.

" is the object of that curious artifice
" and machinery, which she has dif-
" played in all animals? The prefer-
" vation alone of individuals and pro-
" pagation of the species. It seems
" enough for her purpose, if such a rank
" be barely upheld in the universe,
" without any care or concern for the
" happiness of the members that com-
" pose it. No resource for this pur-
" pose: no machinery in order merely
" to give pleasure or ease: no fund of
" pure joy and contentment: no in-
" dulgence, without some want or ne-
" cessity accompanying it. At least the
" phenomena of this nature are over-
" balanced by opposite phenomena of
" still greater importance. Our sense
" of music harmony and indeed beauty
" of all kinds gives satisfaction, without
" being absolutely necessary to the pre-
" servation and propagation of the spe-
" cies. But what racking pains, on the
" other hand, arise from gouts, gravels,
" megrims,

" megrims, tooth-achs, rheumatifms ;
" where the injury to the animal-ma-
" chinery is either fmall or incurable?
" Mirth, laughter, play, frolic feem
" gratuitous fatisfactions, which have
" no farther tendency : Spleen, melan-
" choly, difcontent, fuperftition are
" pains of the fame nature". Again,
(at p. 191.) "You muft at the fame
" time allow, that if pain be lefs fre-
" quent (which is extremely doubtful)
" than pleafure, it is infinitely more vi-
" olent and durable. One hour of it is
" often able to out-weigh a day, a week,
" a month of our common infipid en-
" joyments; And how many days,
" weeks, and months are paffed by ma-
" ny in the moft acute torments? Plea-
" fure fcarcely in one inftance is ever
" able to reach ecftafy and rapture: And
" in no one inftance can it continue
" for any time at its higheft pitch and
" altitude, The fpirits evaporate; the
" nerves relax; the fabric is difordered;
                              " and

PART "and the enjoyment quickly degene-
I. " rates into fatigue and uneafinefs.
" But pain, often, good God, how of-
" ten ! rifes to torture and agony; and
" the longer it continues, it becomes
" ftill more genuine agony and torture.
" Patience is exhaufted ; courage lan-
" guifhes; melancholy feizes us; and no-
" thing terminates our mifery but the
" removal of its caufe, or another event,
" which is the fole cure of all evil, but
" which, from our natural folly, we re-
" gard with ftill greater horror and con-
" fternation". Let us analyfe this tale
of woe. It pofitively afferts, at fetting
out "that the fole object (pray mark
the expreffion "fole") of nature's curious machinery is the prefervation of
individuals and the propagation of the
fpecies". At the diftance of a few fen-
tences, however, the tale enumerates
feveral fources of delight "not abfo-
lutely neceffary to the prefervation and
propagation of the fpecies". Is this
rea-

reafoning, Philo, or prating? would Part
not a fingle inftance (you recite feve- 1.
ral) of "gratuitous fatisfaction" completely exclude the fuppofition of a
total infenfibility and unfeelingnefs, if
we may fo fpeak, in the determinations
of nature? She does not, you fay,
grant as much as I could reafonably
wifh—But, if fhe had been perfectly and
entirely inattentive to your accommodation, would fhe have granted any
thing at all? "The phenomena of her
gracioufnefs, you reply, are overba-
lanced by oppofite phenomena of ftill
greater importance". How does this
fubterfuge demonftrate your firft doctrine of a total uniform obduracy? If
nature had been fo unequivocally void
of goodnefs as you pretend, fhe would
have expofed you to the evils you de-
fcribe without any, the flighteft mix-
ture of alleviation: fhe would never
have imparted any folace, that could
poffibly have been difpenfed with: and
you

PART you would have drunk from her cup
1.   nothing but dregs. You muſt ſurely
retract your firſt accuſation.

DISLODGED from this poſt you next
retreat to the poſition, that evil does,
upon the whole, predominate in the
canvaſs of nature: the picture is caſt
in ſhades. Before we adopt your re-
preſentation, let us ſurvey the facts on
which it is grounded. Your own catalogue of evils is nearly equal in point
of number, with your liſt of bleſſings.
Thus far your argument looks almoſt
equally both ways: it will quickly, I
hope, ſet its face againſt you. If, for
inſtance, your evils, though rather
more numerous than your bleſſings,
be found to center in a comparatively
ſmall number of individuals, while
your bleſſings are pretty generally dif-
fuſed through the human race, there
will evidently reſult, in regard to the
whole creation, a far greater meaſure
of

of happinefs, than of mifery. This PART
conclufion cannot be denied, if the 1.
two firft branches of the fentence are
eftablifhed. To eftablifh them is my
tafk—In regard to the firft branch,
namely, the comparatively narrow operation of PHILO's evils; are moft of
thofe evils, let us afk, any thing elfe
than various fpecies of ill health? And
is health or ficknefs, let us next afk,
the moft ufual vifitant to the fons of
men? A great proportion of mankind
in every civilized country live in a ftate
of idlenefs: if a great part of the remainder was fick, how could the bufinefs of the world go on? Let every
one, in a word, from his own experience ftrike an eftimate of the actual
balance between ficknefs and health,
and then anfwer my queftion, PHILO
has, it muft be confeffed, two evils,
difcontent and fuperftition, not ftrictly
reducible to the head of ficknefs. Are
not both thefe evils, however, of a
very

PART very precarious, fluctuating nature?
I. Chearful company, a fine day, the
flighteft amufement, the moft trivial
employment fufpend, fometimes cure,
their influence. May they not therefore fairly be confidered as a fort of
neutral powers; hanging at equal di-
ftances between the attractions of pleafure and pain, and not decifively gra-
vitating towards either? PHILO's evils,
upon the whole, appear evidently to
have a much more contracted range in
human life than PHILO was willing to
afcribe to them—Let us next fee, if
PHILO's bleffings (which is the fecond
branch of the fentence I am to demonftrate) do not move in a pretty large
circle? Is any man fo unfortunate, as
not frequently to have tafted fome of
thefe bleffings? Is any man fo forlorn,
as to defpair of all future accefs to the
rich feaft?—The reader does, I flatter
myfelf, by this time think me entitled
to the conclufion, which I drew from
o the

the two branches of my fentence now Part
difcuffed, viz. That good, not evil, is i.
the leading feature in the ftate of
mortal affairs.

But though Philo fhould allow
pleafure to have the afcendancy, in
point of frequency, over pain; Philo
ftill laments (p. 191 and 192) that the
former fenfation is inferior to the
latter both in duration and degree.
" Pleafure, he cryes, fcarcely in any
" inftance is ever able to reach ecftafy and
" rapture". What a complaint from a
Philofopher! who tells us (at p. 259)
of thefe very dialogues " That there
" is no ftate of mind fo happy as the
" calm and equable." Without however
preffing the Philofopher either with
his character or declarations, let us
look abroad into the world, and fee
whether the want of "ecftafy and rapture" be very generally and ferioufly
deplored. That part of mankind,
                    B   which

PART which is engaged in conftant employ-
I.   ment, and which poffeffes at the fame
time either a competence or at worft a
bare fufficiency of neceffarys, compre-
hends probably near two thirds, at all
events half of the human race. Now
amongft this very large body it is
much to be doubted if the fcarcity of
"ecftafy and rapture" has, ever fince
the creation, been the tranfient occafion
of a fingle figh. Thefe contented
mortals dream not of raptures, but en-
joy fatisfaction: they have not the
word ecftafy in their mouths, but fo-
lid tranquility in their hearts: they
wifh not to be angels, and are happy
men: they have not yet fchooled them-
felves into difcontent: nor learnt the
fublime fcience of becoming metaphy-
fically miferable——PHILO's eftimate
of pain now claims our attention.
"Pain, often, good God, how often!
" rifes to torture and agony". That
pain is fometimes exceffive, it is more
our

our bufinefs to lament, than to deny. Let us mark however, for the confolation of mankind, that this melancholy grievance appears often of greater magnitude and in far larger dimenfions to the fpectator, than to the fufferer. Perfons, condemned by ficknefs to lafting confinement and quick returns of pain, wear, not uncommonly very ftrong marks of ferenity and acquiefcence. The goodnefs of God's providence infufes, no doubt, fome drops of comfort into the bitter draught of agony, to attemper its malignity and reftrain its exceffive operation.—At the worft, an event, not far diftant from any of us, is, according even to Philo's account (p. 192), "A cure of all evil." Philo indeed adds, "But which, from our natural "folly, we regard with horror and con-"fternation." But pray, if death be really a cure of all evil, are we not, when it comes, cured by it, whether

we

Part
I.

we wifhed to be fo, or not? does death, when it actually takes place, lofe its efficacy, as a remedy, through our pievious mifconceptions of its nature? —Let us here remark, that when men of fenfe fhudder at death, their emotion, it is to be feared, arifes more from depravity, than folly. The profligate and irreligious may naturally recoil from the approach of that futurity whofe reality they have queftioned; and may juftly dread the frowns of that being whofe authority they have defied. But thoufands of virtuous men in all ages have received, and will doubtlefs, to the end of time continue to receive the final fummons of their Creator with calm undifturbed compofure.

PHILO from (p. 199 to p. 102) repeatedly echoes to us, that the whole fublunary fcene (human life of courfe included) wears no ftamp or fignature of

of a benevolent author. This idea (at PART
p. 201) fprouts up into the following I.
allufion. "Did I fhow you a houfe
" or palace, where there was not one
" apartment convenient or agreeable;
" where the windows, doors, fires, paf-
" fages, ftairs and the whole œconomy
" of the building were the fource of
" noife, confufion, fatigue, darknefs
" and the extremes of heat and cold,
" you would certainly blame the con-
" trivance without any farther exami-
" nation." Inftead of examining his
imaginary building, let us afk PHILO a
fimple queftion, namely, whether he
has already entirely forgot "the fenfe
" of mufic harmony and beauty?" of p.
187. "The mirth, laughter, play,
" frolic" of p. 188? Has, in a word, the
whole fair train of "gratuitous fatisfactions," enumerated by himfelf, totally efcaped from his recollection? If
a fingle trace of them had furvived in
his memory, he would furely not have

reple-

PART reprefented his miferable allegorical
 I.   lodging fo fhockingly ill-furnifhed, fo
completely deficient in every, the fmalleft, article of accommodation.

FROM p. 205 to p. 217 PHILO employs himfelf in difplaying four circumftances, on which, to ufe his own
words p. 203, "All or the greateft
" part of the ills that moleft fenfible
" creatures depend" and by the removal of which the creation would, in
his conception (p. 217.) be prodi-
gioufly improved. — Notwithftanding
however PHILO's prefent apparent acquiefcence in his new mundane arrangements, we find him, no farther off
than p. 218, ftaggering into the following reflexion, "Shall we fay that thefe
" circumftances are not neceffary, and
" that they might eafily have been
" altered in the contrivance of the
" univerfe? This decifion feems too
" prefumptuous for creatures fo blind
" and

"and ignorant." What a pity, Philo, is it, that this very natural obvious fentiment did not occur to you, a
few pages back, at your firft entrance
into the intricacys of cofmogonic cri-
ticifm! How endlefs is it to object
to what we do not underftand! How
idle is the propofal of altering what
we do not know if we can improve!
To erect card-conftructed houfes indeed with the infant, to weave ftraw-
crowns with the maniac feem far more
rational employments of time and in-
tellect than for blind mortals to revife
creation, and ignorant theorifts to new-
model the univerfe.

Descending then from thefe illu-
five, air-built fpeculations, let us haften
to the final refult of all the foregoing
theories, namely, to Philo's reprefentation, inferred from the faid theories, of the divine attributes.

Philo's

PART   PHILO's firſt poſition on this head
  I.   (p. 221.) runs thus, "There may four
       " hypotheſes be framed concerning the
       " firſt cauſes of the univerſe: that they
       " are endowed with perfect goodneſs :
       " that they have perfect malice: that
       " they are oppoſite and have both
       " goodneſs and malice: that they have
       " neither goodneſs nor malice : mixt
       " phenomena can never prove the two
       " former principles : and the unifor-
       " mity and ſteadineſs of general laws
       " ſeems to oppoſe the third ; the fourth
       " therefore, ſeems by far the moſt pro-
       " bable." In oppoſition however to
     the fourth ſuppoſal, let it be aſked,
     whether one ſingle ſolitary inſtance
     (Philo has recounted ſeveral) of " gra-
     tuitous ſatisfaction," would not forbid
     us to conſider the Deity as abſolutely
     regardleſs of our welfare? Let it next
     be remarked, that to thoſe, who adopt
     my eſtimate of human happineſs and
     miſery, the belief of God's benevolence
                                          ac-

acquires inftant confirmation, and Part
ftands erected upon a fair ample, im- I.
moveable foundation.

Philo's next feature in the divine
nature is thus fketched (p. 222.)
" What I have faid concerning natural
" evil will apply to moral, with little
" or no variation; we have no more
" reafon to infer, that the rectitude of
" the fupreme being refembles human
" rectitude than that his benevolence
" refembles the human." In fubverfion
of this doctrine I will beg leave to cite
a paffage from " Mr. Hume's 11th
effay on the practical confequences of
natural religion," where Epicurus, in
a fpeech afcribed to him (p. 217.) thus
expreffes himfelf, " I acknowledge that
" in the prefent order of things virtue
" is attended with much more peace of
" mind than vice, and meets with a more
" favourable reception in the world. I am
" fenfible, that according to the paft ex-
" perience

" perience of mankind, friendſhip is the
" chief joy of human life, moderation the
" only ſource of tranquility and happi-
" neſs. I never balance between the
" virtuous and vicious courſe of life; but
" am ſenſible, that to a well diſpoſed mind
" every advantage is on the ſide of the
" former." The ſupreme being then, has
(by the confeſſion of a perſon not to be
ſuſpected of bigotry) interwoven in the
very frame and conſtitution of things,
a teſtimony to the ſuperiority of virtue
above vice : in other words, the Al-
mighty hath provided, that the prefe-
rence due to the former quality beyond
the latter, ſhould be ſuggeſted to us, at
every ſtep of our exiſtence, by the
ſtriking evidence of familiar facts.
With this glaring document of the deity's love for moral uprightneſs in us,
let us couple PHILO's aſſertion, (p. 236.)
that the nature of the ſupreme being
does, in point of intelligence, " bear a
" confiderable reſemblance to ours." And
will

will this nature, in the direction of its PART
inteligence, totally renounce the rules   I.
recommended by itfelf for the government of our analogous intelligence? fhall
the declared lover of righteoufnefs not
do right? fhall the determined patron
of juftice be himfelf unjuft?

PART

PART II.

PHILO opens his charge (p.243.) againſt religion with the following invective. " How happens it then, if " vulgar ſuperſtition * be ſo ſalutary to ſociety

* What PHILO means by vulgar ſuperſtition may be learnt from p. 244. CLEANTHES there remarks, " That when religion diſtinguiſhes itſelf and acts as a " ſeparate principle over men, it has departed from its " proper ſphere, and has become only a cover to faction " and ambition." To this PHILO replies " And ſo will " all religion, except the philoſophical and rational." All religion then, according to PHILO, except the philoſophical and rational will become the cover to faction and ambition. To be the cover of faction and ambition is, in the ordinary acceptation of the words, to be the ſource of all the miſchiefs aſcribed to vulgar ſuperſtition in the preſent page. All religion therefore, except the philoſophical and rational, is evidently, in PHILO's view of things, vulgar ſuperſtition.

The profeſſors of philoſophical religion are ſaid (p. 261)

PART
II.

" fociety, that all hiftory abounds fo
" much with accounts of its pernicious
" confequences on public affairs? fac-
" tions, civil wars, perfecutions, fubver-
" fions of government, oppreffion, flave-
" ry; thefe are the difmal confequences
" which always attend its prevalency
" over the minds of men. If the religi-
" ous fpirit be ever mentioned in any hi-
" ftorical narration, we are fure to meet
" afterwards with a detail of the miferies
" which attend it." We fhall be extreme-
" ly miftaken, if we confider all the mif-
" chiefs

261) to be extremely few. The faith of thefe profeffors is reprefented (at p. 262) as centering entirely
in one folitary fpeculative tenet, which (to ufe the
very words there employed in characterizing it) " af-
" fords no inference that can affect human life, or can
" be the fource of any action or forbearance," fo fimple
a code of divinity can evidently not incumber its pro-
felytes with temples, modes of worfhip, or fear of hea-
venly power. The profeffors of this pure theology are
of courfe eafy to be diftinguifhed. Thefe pure theo-
logifts, once diftinguifhed, negatively afcertain to us
the vulgarly fuperftitious part of mankind, namely,
all other perfons, except atheifts, and thefe contempla-
tive fingle-teneted religionifts.

chiefs in which the word religion has PART
been held out, or in which religionifts   II.
had concern, as the genuine fruit of
mere religious influence. The name
of religion has often hung upon the
tongue, where no particle of her holy
energy reached the heart. PHILO
himfelf will inform us (p. 244.) that
" religion is (only) a cover to faction
" and ambition," which are the real
prompters of thofe turbulent fcenes
where religion alone appears upon the
ftage. Now ambition and faction are
durable permanent principles; and, if
religion had never exifted, would undoubtedly, on fome pretence or other,
have found vent. Paffions, in a word,
that ufe religion fimply as a veil, will,
though ftriped of the veil, prefent an
undaunted front : though detected,
they will not be difmayed. Ambition and
faction are no bigots. Divefted of
their religious difguife, they inftantly
affume fome other; immediately new-

u   drefs

PART drefs their indefatigable characters, nor
II.   remain a fingle moment abfent fiom
the ftage They fubftitute perhaps
popularity for prayers; Agrarian laws
for alms; and largeffes to the mob inftead of donations to faints. — They
have, it is true, often borrowed the
vizor of religion; muft religion therefore be made their voucher? muft that
chafte and holy principle be loaded
with the infamy of actions, which fhe
had not the fmalleft concern in giving
birth to? muft fhe be rendered refpon-
fible for meafures, which fhe was not
allowed to direct; and be reprefented as
the advifer of thofe, by whom fhe was
never confulted? — What? — Some
men have bafely proftituted the name
of religion, all men therefore ought to
renounce her precepts! fome perfons,
not really under her guidance, have
acted wrong, fhe muft therefore no
longer teach us to act right! We muft
ftrip ourfelves of the fubftance, becaufe
others

others have put on the femblance. PART
Religion, in fine, having been accom- II.
modated to bad ends, muft on that account, not be permitted to promote
good ones*. By this mode of reafoning
the worthy man, whofe fignature is
counterfeited for the purpofes of forgery,
ought to fuffer capital punifhment:
and honefty, becaufe perfonated now
and then by hypocrify, fhould be pro-
fcribed as a fpecies of villany.

PHILO (p. 243.) declares pofitively
that "no periods of time can be happier
"or more profperous than thofe in
"which it (religion) is never heard of
"nor regarded." Before we affent to
this propofition, let us recollect, that
at no period probably of time whatever
was religion fo little heard of or regarded, as in the æra immediately preceding
the diffolution of the Roman republick.

               C   — In

* The ineftimable benefits refulting from religion
will be difplayed in a fubfequent paragraph

PART
II.

—In this immaculate æra (let us briefly trace its happiness and prosperity) one man concerted and had nearly executed a general massacre of the supreme magistrates, with a total subversion of a free government. — Governors of extensive provinces constantly ravaged the unhappy objects of their jurisdiction, with merciless, and more than hostile licentiousness. — Fortunes of an almost imperial amplitude, vanished daily at the touch of dissipation: while, to repair the mighty ruins, crimes of every complexion and enormity were, without fear or compunction, had recourse to — one general alone, in pursuit of wealth and power, desolated Gaul, threw his own country into convulsions, nor finished his career till near two millions of his fellow-creatures had fallen victims to his ambition.— Can one meditate without horror on almost any of the principal transactions in PHILO's golden age religion

religion had indubitably no concern in
thofe dreadful fcenes: and may fecurely
exclaim in the language of our Poet;
" Thou canft not fay, I did it " ——
Let us now fuppofe for a moment,
that religion had actually happened to
have interefted, in Philo's favorite
age, the paffions of mankind. What
would have been the confequence? fhe
would, in all human probability, have
been appointed the nominal prefident,
the oftenfible high-prieftefs at the
dreadful rites. Cæsar would have
been a Cromwell : would have waved
a dagger in one hand, his manual in
the other · would have pretended,
while he fought only his own aggran-
difement, " to feek the Lord *.   If this
imaginary ftate of things indeed had
really taken place; religion, we may
be affured, would have been marked by
Philo, as principal inftigatrefs of

C 2   Cæsar's

* A favorite expreffion of Cromwell.

PART
II.

CÆSAR's worſt actions, as the ſole mover of his way-ward ambition!

PHILO proceeds (p. 244.) to depreciate the efficacy of futuie rewards and puniſhments. " The inference is not " juſt, becauſe finite rewards and pu- " niſhments have ſo great influence, " that therefore ſuch as aie infinite " and eternal muſt have ſo much " greater. Conſider, I beſeech you, " the attachment we have to preſent " things, and the little concern we diſ- " cover for objects ſo remote and un- " certaiı. When divines are declaim- " ing againſt the common behaviour " and practice of the world, they al- " ways repreſent this principle as the " ſtrongeſt imaginable (which indeed " it is) and deſcribe almoſt all human " kind as lying under the influence of " it, and ſunk into the deepeſt lethargy " and unconcern about their religious " intereſts. Yet theſe ſame divines, " when

" when they refute their fpeculative
" antagonifts, fuppofe the motives of
" religion to be fo powerful, that,
" without them, it were impoffible for
" civil fociety to fubfift; nor are they
" afhamed of fo palpable a contradic-
" tion." They need not PHILO, be
afhamed of it, for it is not, (if my conjectures are right) a contradiction. The
meaning of the divines (if I could be
referred to their works) would prove,
I really believe, confiftent. It probably
runs thus, fenfible objects, take ftrong
and lafting hold of the human mind;
and powerfully detach it from the doctrines of eternity: the doctrines of
eternity however, by means of exhor-
tation and meditation, do in many inftances find entrance into the heart,
once admitted they operate potently;
mightily convert the inclinations; and
prevent numberlefs enormities. Without
their falutary influence, fociety would
be deluged with infufferable profligacy;

and

PART
II.
and be rendered incapable of fubfifting.
— In oppofition to thefe very rational
fuggeftions of the divines, PHILO remarks (p. 245.)   " It is certain from
" experience, that the fmalleft grain of
" natural honefty and benevolence, has
" more effect on men's conduct, than
" the moft pompous views fuggefted by
" theological theories and fyftems."
Suppofing, though not admitting, the
truth of this pofition, how PHILO does
it anfwer your prefent purpofe? in
what fhape does it conftitute a plea for
the entire difcardure of religion? in re-
commending the exterminating fyftem,
'tis your bufinefs to prove — not, that
religion has little influence : but, that
fhe has none at all. This latter pofition
however, you will fcarce venture abfo-
lutely to maintain, after having declared (p.246.) that religion " operates
by ftarts and bounds," that is, that
religion has fome influence: — calcu-
late PHILO, the amount of this influence

ence at your difcretion : does it direct one half, one third, or one fourth of human agency? deliver your eftimate. Morality will accept it at your hands; and rejoice in the friendly tender. SAUL flew his thoufands, DAVID his ten thoufands; yet, both furely merited the applaufe of their countrymen. Is the general, who wins five battles, to be difgraced, becaufe another general wins ten? no judicious perfon, in a word, will, in the great tafk of curbing human wickednefs, reject any, the very flighteft, co-operation. — Aware perhaps of fome reafoning of this kind PHILO employs, (p. 246.) in ftill farther difparaging the energy of the religious principle : reprefenting it as an inert, lifelefs fpring of action; a monitor, eafy to be filenced; a lawgiver, without difficulty eluded; an advifer whom no one pays more attention to, than paffion and inclination permit.—Fully to convince us indeed,

C 4   that

PART that the caput mortuum of religion
II. may be eafily difpenfed with in fociety,
PHILO peremptorily afferts (p. 247.)
that " none but fools ever repofe lefs
" truft in a man, becaufe they hear,
" that from ftudy and philofophy, he has
" entertained fome fpeculative doubts
" on theological fubjects." Notwithftanding this teftimonial to the inno-
cency and uprightnefs of irreligion;
which perfon, in the name of common
fenfe, is moft worthy of confidence
and dependance; the man, who is re-
ftrained folely by a regard to character
and intereft : or the man, who in ad-
dition to the above motives, has the
controul likewife of divine vengeance,
hanging inceffantly, like DAMOCLES's
fword, over his every procedure ?

PHILO, not content with detracting
from the influence of religion in the
article of enforcing virtue, proceeds to
accufe her of encouraging vice — The
firft

firſt ſpecies of proof, employed by Part
Philo in the ſupport of his bold II.
charge, is the exhibition of certain
odious, unworthy religious characters.
" When we have to do (p. 247) with
" a man, who makes a great profeſſion
" of religion and devotion; has this
" any other effect upon ſeveral, who
" paſs for prudent, than to put them on
" their guard, leſt they be cheated and
" deceived by him?" Again (p. 248)
" Amongſt ourſelves ſome have been
" guilty of that atrocioufneſs, unknown
" to the Grecian and Egyptian ſuper-
" ſtitions, of declaiming, in expreſs
" terms, againſt morality." The figure of " pars pro toto," though tole-
rated in compoſition, is intolerable in
argument. Philo, in the paſſages before us, points out certain reprehen-
fible characters, by no means predominant in the religious Drama, and
repreſents them as the principal actors.
He would, no doubt, wiſh us to ima-
gine,

PART
II.

gine, that the Pharifaical Hypocrite in the firft extract, and the unprincipled enthufiaft in the fecond are faithful famples of the generality of religionifts: that they have the true family-face; and may ferve as models of their brethren.

AT p. 248. PHILO launches at religion the following invective, "Even "though fuperftition or enthufiafm "fhould not put itfelf in direct oppo- "fition to morality; the very divert- "ing of the attention, the raifing up "a new and frivolous fpecies of merit, "the prepofterous diftribution which "it makes of praife and blame, muft "have the moft pernicious confe- "quences, and weaken extremely men's "attachment to the natural motives "of juftice and humanity." Let us here paufe; and beftow a thorough examination upon that "new frivolous "fpecies of merit" practical religion: let

let us afcertain its intrinfic value: let PART
us enquire, if the pretended mafs of   II.
drofs wear not an imperial fuperfcrip-
tion; be not ftamped with a divine
image.

FOR the origin of religion I fhall
appeal folely to the authority * of Mr.
HUME; who (in his differtation on the
natural hiftory of religion, fect. 4. p.
24,) remarks " That the only point
" of theology, in which we fhall find a
" confent of mankind almoft univer-
" fal, is, that there is invifible, intel-
" ligent power in the world." Again,
(fect. 15. p. 114.) " The univerfal
" propenfity to believe in invifible, in-
" telligent power, if not an original
" inftinct, being at leaft a general at-
" tendant of human nature, it may be
" confidered as a kind of mark or
                              " ftamp,

* Better authority might, doubtlefs, be produced:
but none, probably, fo fatisfactory to PHILO.

PART "ftamp, which the divine workman
II. "has fet upon his work — Before we
proceed to decypher this heaven-im-
printed character, this hand-writing,
as it were, of nature; let us ftep back
for a moment, to the dialogues, and
liften to PHILO, haranguing (at p.
228) in the following ftrain," "*That*
" *nature does nothing in vain*, is a max-
" im eftablifhed in all the fchools,
" merely from the contemplation of
" the works of nature, without any
" religious purpofe; and, from a firm
" conviction of its truth, an anato-
" mift who had obferved a new organ
" or canal, would never be fatisfied
" till he had alfo difcovered its ufe and
" intention." The all-fagacious ar-
chitect has therefore, furely, not *in
vain* implanted in our nature the religious propenfity: nor fwerved in this
fingle important inftance from her
ufual maxims of providence. Let us
now then endeavour to unfold her
counfels

counfels in this particular: and develop, PART
as far as we are able, the "ufe and in-   II.
" tention" or final caufe, as it is often
called, of religion * — The human
body, it has been repeatedly obferved,
is incapable of perpetual exertion.
Certain paufes are occafionally requi-
fite to relieve the ftrained machine, and
readjuft its difordered fprings. All
nations accordingly, without exception, have invariably indulged them-
felves in periodical feafons of relax-
ation — A ftate of inactivity, let it
next be remarked, is to men in general, particularly to the lower orders of
our fpecies a ftate of danger. The
human mind no fooner ftagnates, than
it putrefies — How fortunate then
would it be, if mankind could be engaged,

---

* Though my conjectures on this momentous fubject fhould not be deemed fatisfactory, ftill let it be
remembered, that the religious propenfity, according
to the well-founded maxim of the fchools quoted by
PHILO, indifputably has a final caufe.

a

Part gaged, during part of their day of reft
ii.   in fome innocent employment; which
      might fill up fome intervals of a very
      perilous feafon unexceptionably; and
      render leifure, the fource of mifchief,
      in fome degree innoxious! But how
      would our fatisfaction redouble, if the
      much-wifhed for employment fhould
      prove not fimply inoffenfive; but
      fhould confift in calling mankind to-
      gether * to the performance of offices
      of a compofed, folemn, awful caft;
      replete with ftilnefs and fobriety; and
      calculated to fettle the heart into a
      falutary calm. The effect of fuch a
      foul-fteadying exercife would furely not
      be entirely momentary; but would fol-
      low the mind probably beyond the
      walls of the temple; and fortify it for
      fome time, againft the fuggeftions of
                                    idle

---

* Mere affociation, if regulated by decorum, has
a moft efficacious tendency, in the opinion of intelligent judges, to civilize and polifh the human race.

idle levity. To an avocation of the PART
kind here defcribed can every religion II.
under heaven perhaps boaft itfelf to
amount—But if paganifm be all this,
what is not Chriftianity? In the religious affemblies of thofe regions, where
the celeftial ray of revelation fhines
with free luftre, we fhall hear a hea-
ven-defcended performance conftantly
recited, pregnant with the pureft maxims of morality, and rich in interefting
difplays of future exiftence — The very
prayers too, in the well-conftructed
religious affemblies of thofe regions,
will not merely implore divine protection; but will, in doing fo, briefly recall to view, the moft effectual recom-
mendation to divine protection, moral
excellency — The perfuafions of a
holy orator will, at the clofe, reinforce
the general impreffion. From fuch a
fertile field of inftruction, from fuch a
matchlefs fchool of morality, what bar-
barian can depart totally unmeliorated?

There

Part
II.
There is no one, I firmly believe, scarcely the moſt hardened, but what carries away from the religious meetings of true proteſtantiſm ſome degree of improvement, ſome ſenſe of duty. Suppoſe, with Philo, this improvement, this ſenſe of duty "to operate "by ſtarts and bounds," to prevent bad actions only occaſionally, at particular ſeaſons: ſtill will the benefit reſulting from them be great, ſuperlative, and ineſtimable!

But Philo entertains quite different conceptions; and maintains religion to be the parent of evil, rather than of good: more a friend to vice, than virtue — The inſtance of the bad tendency of religion, produced by Philo at p. 249, carries a very ſtriking peculiar air. "Many religious exerciſes are "entered into with ſeeming fervour, "where the heart at the time, feels cold "and languid: a habit of diſſimula-
tion

"tion is by degrees contracted: and fraud
"and falfhood become the predominant
"principle." Concife piece of demon-
ftration! A man performs certain religious offices negligently — is rendered
by that means a hypocrite — quickly
after a complete rogue! when fuch
unbounded licentioufnefs of inference
is freely and unblufhingly practifed,
there feems to be no reafon, why one
man, as well as another, may not pre-
fume to draw conclufions. I will try
therefore, if from the fame premifes,
which have afforded Philo fo much
fcandalous deduction againft religion,
I cannot derive a pofition of a diffimi-
lar and perfectly oppofite nature. From
Philo's premife then at the beginning
of the above extract I reafon, as fol-
lows: A confcioufnefs of the defcribed
infirmity throws the religionift into a
ftate of humiliation, proftration of foul,
and abafement—which penitential e-
motions foon terminate in their cogenial

D   habi-

PART habitudes lowlinefs, and Chriftian
II. meeknefs —— PHILO, in the concluding fentence of p. 249. carries on his
lately-fabricated religious hypocrite
through the fiery regions "of the high-
" eft zeal in religion and the deepeft
" hypocrify" till, in the firft paragraph of p. 250. the wretch is calcined
into " an enthufiaftic zealot whom no
" morality can be forcible enough to
" bind." That fuch mifcreants, as are
here exhibited, have exifted, no candid
perfon will deny: but mark: PHILO can
reap not the leaft benefit from the con-
ceffion, till he prove the generality of
religionifts to be of a fimilar diabolical
ftamp — PHILO here, as upon a former occafion, lets loofe upon us the
figure of " Pars pro toto": a moft pal-
try, furely, exceptionable, and inade-
quate engine of perfuafion.

IN the fecond paragraph of p. 250.
PHILO brings forward a moft unheard-
of

of accufation againft religion, com-
plaining "That the fteady attention
" alone to fo important an intereft as
" that of eternal falvation, is apt to
" extinguifh the benevolent affections,
" and beget a narrow, contracted felf-
" ifhnefs."   Rather, will not the contemplation of fo truly interefting an
objeft as immortal blifs abforp, as it
were, the foul; fwallow up all its lower attachments; and completely difen-
gage it from the attraction of thofe
fublunary concerns in which felfifhnefs
and   narrow-mindednefs   principally
center?

I SHALL entirely pafs over PHILO's
reflections (p. 251 and 252.) upon the
degree of afcendancy and influence,
proper to be allowed the priefthood.
A difcuffion of thefe topics would
not materially affect, fo far as I can
judge, the fubject in debate; which is
the native excellence and general good

tend-

PART tendency of religion. These attributes
II. of religion, if proved, muft eternally
remain unfullied, unaltered, unimpair-
ed; neither fympathizing with political
arrangements; nor fufceptible of tar-
nifh from the mifconduct of particular
priefts.

IT has often been urged in favour
of religion, that it gives efficacy to
oaths. To invalidate this plea, PHILO
firft (p. 253) reprefents feveral circumftances (perfectly independant of religion) as forming "the chief reftraint"
upon a fwearer's tongue. That the
circumftances, enumerated by PHILO,
have a tendency to enforce truth in
depofitions, we allow. But has not
religion a fimilar tendency, in an infinitely greater degree? PHILO infinuates,
that fhe has little or none!—In farther
fupport of his hypothefis, PHILO ap-
prizes us (p. 253) "That cuftom-
" houfe oaths and political oaths are
but

" but little regarded even by fome who
" pretend to principles of honefty and
" religion." From this fact Philo
wifhes us, probably, to reafon in the
following manner: An appeal is equally made to heaven, in cuftom-houfe
oaths and political oaths, as in other
oaths of a more valid nature: the more
valid oaths therefore do evidently not
derive their validity from that appeal
to heaven, which belongs, in an equal
degree, to them, and to the invalid
cuftom-houfe or political oath.　To
this fuggeftion let us thus reply; The
contempt in which many perfons hold
the rights of the public, * in compari-
fon with the rights of individuals, may

D 3　　　eafily

---

* The interefts of the community are certainly,
though one fcarce knows upon what ground, deemed
far lefs facred by the generality of mankind, than the
rights of individuals.　Many perfons, for inftance,
of unqueftionable honefty in private concerns, will,
without fhame or fcruple, engage in the purchafe or
difpofal of contraband commodities, though fuch
practices are palpable, indifputable frauds upon the
interefts of the community.

PART eafily lead fuch wrong-headed cafuifts
II. to conceive, that an appeal to heaven,
in regard to the former, is lefs noticed
by the moft High, than when it relates
to the latter branch of rights. Thefe
motley moralifts, therefore, while they
lay no ftrefs upon the infpection of omni-
fcience in public, may poffibly be greatly
influenced by a fenfe of it in private depofitions: may, in a word, partially elude,
while they by no means totally abjure
the belief of celeftial cognizance in the
tranfaction of fwearing — Let us farther remark, that the generality of
religionifts would, it is to be hoped,
recoil from the crime of perjury in one
fcene, no lefs than in another: at the
cuftom-houfe, equally as in a court
of judicature — PHILO's next furmife,
(p. 253) in derogation to the utility
of religion in atteftations, is founded
upon the validity of a Quaker's alleve-
ration. PHILO means, no doubt, by
this inftance, to intimate, that veracity
is

is attainable in depofitions, without Part
the help of religious enforcements. An II.
examination however of the fact ad-
duced will decifively forbid any fuch
inference. From what, may we afk,
does a Quaker's obftinate adherence to
the fcheme of fimple affeveration proceed, but from an extreme veneration
for the authority of fcripture? Now
the fame fcripture, which teaches the
Quaker, through the medium of erro-
neous conftruction, never to exceed the
line of fimple affirmation, does more
clearly and more explicitly teach him
never, in his affirmation, to exceed the
line of truth. A Quaker's affeveration,
is therefore, we may well conclude,
often purified by a recollection of
fcriptural precepts: its veracity, in a
word, refults, in no fmall degree, from
the influence of religious impreffion.
— Philo next endeavours to gainfay
that opinion of Polybius, which af-
cribes the infamy of Greek faith to
D 4   the

PART the prevalency of the EPICUREAN phi-
II. lofophy. "But I know alfo (replies
"PHILO p. 254) that PUNIC faith had
"as bad a reputation in ancient times,
"as IRISH evidence has in modern;
"though we cannot account for thefe
"vulgar obfervations by the fame rea-
"fon." But what? Becaufe a com-
mercial fpirit of avarice, or any other
caufe unknown to us, has accidentally
engendered habits of perjury; do irreligious tenets on that account, ceafe
to produce a fimilar effect? Avarice
frequently inftigates men to difhonefty,
therefore ambition does not. An ordinary fire yields heat, *therefore* the fun
affords none.—PHILO makes one ftrug-
gle more (p. 254) to enervate POLY-
BIUS's conjecture; attempting to convince us, from a paffage in EURIPIDES,
"That Greek faith was infamous be-
"fore the rife of the EPICUREAN phi-
"lofophy." Without entering into a
difcuffion of the paffage in EURIPIDES,
let

let us peremptorily and determinately Part
object to touches of poetry, as com-   II.
petent evidence of national manners.
A fingle well known inftance of any
crime, exifting in a perfon whom a poet
wifhes, but is afraid directly to attack,
will eafily give birth to a poetical effufion
of general farcafm, no way expreffive
of general truth : The fole purpofe of
fuch farcafm being to glance upon,
without feeming to aim at fome particular individual ; and to infinuate, not
avowedly point, a private imputation.

Philo (p. 256.) vents the following
murmur; " The terrors of religion
" commonly prevail above its comforts.
" — It is allowed, that men never have
" recourfe to devotion, fo readily as
" when dejected with grief, or depreffed
" with ficknefs. Is not this a proof
" that the religious fpirit is not fo
" nearly allied to joy, as to forrow?"
Let us apply the argumentative procefs
                                    of

PART of this fentiment, to another ftrictly
II. fimilar fet of ideas.—It is allowed that
men never have recourfe to the offices
of friendfhip, fo readily as when dejected
with grief, or oppreffed with ficknefs.
Is not this a full proof that the fpirit
of friendfhip is not fo nearly allied to
joy, as to forrow?—How many things,
or, rather how eafily may any thing be
proved by the admiffion of fuch lax
reafoning?

In p. 257, 258, 259. PHILO lamen s
that the profpects of a future ftate,
exhibited by popular religions, wear
univerfally a difmal, inaufpicious appearance. — Before we object to this
reprefentation, let us briefly remark,
that the reprefentation, though admitted, affords no pretence for the renunciation of religion.   For if religion as
was formerly attempted to be fhown,
refult from a divine impulfe, and produce

duce the moſt extenſive benefits, her Part
authoritative practical ſupremacy will   II.
for ever remain unſhaken, whatever
be the complexion of her future remu-
neratory ſyſtem. Though our attention, in a word, ſhould be unwilling to
follow religion, into the other world, it
will ſtill be our duty and our intereſt
to adhere to her in this. — This being
premiſed, let us now, upon very familiar grounds of exception, expreſs un-
willingneſs to hear a ſingle ſyllable
from Philo, on the ſubject of a future
ſtate. That awful ſcene, like all other
ſcenes of a mixed chequered nature,
is, doubtleſs, viewed in different lights
by different imaginations: chearfulneſs,
ſuppoſing criminality out of the queſtion, fixes on the bright, deſpondency on
the cloudy part of the horizon. To
the gaiety of Philo's temper his picture of human life, examined at the
opening of this performance, bears
ample

PART ample teftimony. A paffage too (in
II. Mr. HUME's differtation on the natural
hiftory of religion) may ferve to throw
farther light upon the complexion of
PHILO's pofthumous meditations. Mr.
HUME (in the paffage alluded to, Sect.
15. p. 115.) remarks, "that the moft
"open impiety is attended with a
"fecret dread and compunction." PHILO
upon the whole, does not feem a perfon, to whom any cool difpaffionate
man, ought to apply for a defcription
of futurity.

PHILO concludes his elaborate declamation againft religion, with inform-
ing us (p. 259.) "That though this
"opinion (about future happinefs
"and mifery) be feldom fo fteady in
"its operation, as to influence all the
"actions; yet it is apt to make a con-
"fiderable breach in the temper, and
"to produce that gloom and melan-
"choly,

" choly, fo remarkable in all devout Part
" people." Philo feems in this paf- ii.
fage, to forget a former piece of information of his, (at p. 246.) " That re-
" ligious motives where they act at all,
" operate only by ftarts and bounds;
" and it is fcarcely poffible for them to
" become altogether habitual to the
" mind."   Religious motives, we fee
(at p. 246.) work only temporary effects : while (at p. 249.) they produce
lafting operations.   Religious motives
indeed, feem in Philo's hands to be
fufceptible, like Milton's angels, of oc-
cafional contraction and dilatation, juft
as circumftances require.   When we
talk of their falutary influence, " They
" act only (Philo tells us) by ftarts
" and bounds."   On a fudden however as foon as Philo himfelf handles
the penfive tendency of thefe narrowly-
operating principles, they fwell on the
imagination ; acquire formidable magnitude;

PART nitude; and "make a confiderable
II.   " breach in the temper." — Without
availing ourfelves of PHILO's inconfift-
ency, without endeavouring to render
the philofopher an evidence againft
himfelf, let us difpaffionately enquire
into the reality of that gloom and
melancholy, afcribed by PHILO to all
devout people.—A fhort appeal on this
topic may firft, with propriety, be
made to the actual experience of mankind. Are religion and chearfulnefs,
in general incompatible? let every
man's perfonal obfervation anfwer the
queftion. — Let us next remark, that
(when the gloom of a religionift arifes,
as in innumerable inftances it certainly
does, from natural temper) the religionift, though gloomy with, would indifputably have been fo without religion.
The unfortunate man carries that
within him, which fpreads an unvary-
ing fhade round his fteps : and which,

if

if not exerted upon religious truth, PART
would undoubtedly faſten on and dif-   II.
colour ſome other objеѐt. — Let us in
the laſt place, aſk PHILO this ſimple,
but material queſtion : whatever be the
nature of the religioniſt's ſorrow, does
PHILO tender him a cure? Has ſcepti-
cal philoſophy any balm to comfort the
devout heart; any medicine to refreſh
the religiouſly-afflicted ſpirit? let us,
in imagination, conſign the religioniſt
to PHILO's direction, and watch the
reſult.—PHILO, it will here be proper
to recollect, launches (at p.244.) into
the following exclamation," conſider,
" I beſeech you, the attachment which
" we have to preſent things, and the
" little concern we diſcover for objects
" ſo remote and uncertain, viz. eternal
" rewards and puniſhments." Apply
this doctrine to the caſe of PHILO's
patient. The unhappy man was melancholy from the contemplation of
                                objects

PART
II.

objects *remote and uncertain*; turned over to PHILO he inftantly hears* fuch a horrid reprefentation of things *prefent*, as will harrow up his foul, and hurry him into the exceffes of phrenfy and defperation. He was anxious while directed by devotion: touched by the wand of infidelity he feels his anxiety redouble, his horrors infinitely accumulate. Under the influence of religion he moped : under the guidance of PHILO he will perhaps deftroy himfelf.

Pol me occidiftis, amici,
Non fervaftis. Hor.

The picture, or rather caricature, of religion, exhibited by PHILO in the dialogues, may perhaps not unhappily be contrafted with a fhort etching of irreligion, which appears in Mr. HUME's dif-

* See PHILO's lamentations over the miferies of life, difcuffed at the beginning of this performance.

differtation on the natural hiftory of PART
religion. Sect. 16. p.116. " Look out   II.
" (cries the great philofopher) for a ⌣⌣
" people entirely devoid of religion:
" If you find them at all, be affured,
" that they are but few degrees remov-
" ed from brutes." To what worfe
ftate, great and good God, can the
ftricteft profeffion of thy holy religion
reduce us!

ERRATA.

P. 19. line 2. for *mark* read *remark*.

30. l. laſt of the text, dele ".

38. l. 14. for *diſcardure* read *renunciation*.

42. l. 8. at the beginning, dele *At*.